OPEN PIT

a story about morococha and extractivism in the américas

OPEN

JOSE ANTONIO VILLARÁN

PIT

Counterpath
Denver and New York
2022

Counterpath
www.counterpathpress.org

ISBN 978-1-93399677-6

Library of Congress Cataloging in Publication Data is available.

CONTENTS

what happens
if the way in which we study reality
is confusing, chaotic?

to inform about the encounter
to write
to show the inconsistency of reality

—eloy neira

the parent writer (0)

the people (0.5in; 1.27cm)

capital (1in; 2.54cm)

the extra-human (1.5in; 3.81cm)

government (2in; 5.08cm)

the actant that's not one of the actants
that forms part of the body of the open pit
(2.5in; 6.35cm)

at least 6 people/actants
2 tables: 1 long, 1 small
6 chairs

the actants can be embodied by folks of any gender, sexuality, race, or age.
the body of the open pit; capital, the people, government, the extra-human and
the parent writer, sits together at the longer table. the actant that's not one of the
actants that forms part of the body of the open pit sits alone at the small table.
each actant should stand up when reading, unless indicated otherwise.

a chinese company
buys a large mining site in perú

copper
molybdenum
and silver deposits run through
the mountain

there's a town on the mountain
a bull with no horns

in order to reach the deposits

the people must go
as must the mountain

       all goes round again

the company claims it won't force
anyone to leave
the craters will reach the town
in eight years

instructions:

the extra-human world exists as background noise and reads slowly and at a slightly lower volume than the other two actants. the text is also meant to be read as a closed loop: the extra-human world returns to the beginning when reaching the end. both the parent and the extra-human actants start reading at the same time. the text ends when the actant that's not one of the actants that forms part of the body of the open pit reads their last line.

*

it starts they start that's their main problem
the notion of a beginning or an end it starts
for them for him we stare at ourselves (a body
without orphans) we're here it starts for them
for him a story always a story all they care for
their own little stories their own little stories
little stories a beginning something to grasp
on no sense of apposition the undercommons
always already it starts for them for him they

want to know things they want to control things
they start drilling we feel it they start drilling
and we feel it they start drilling and we feel it
they start drilling and we feel it

they start
drilling

the story i want rob nixon to write would start with a large bank of
cumulus clouds overlooking an open pit mine wedged between a
fractured mountain range, the sun would be setting as a family of
seven guides a small herd of goats towards the nearest water basin.

no, that's not right

a large conference, a crowded auditorium, hundreds of
people, cameras, microphones, a certain thickness to the
air, deloitte's ceo is giving a presentation on the most
important mining trends for the coming year.

i can't stop thinking about the fact that you can now perceive light.

he'll be born in six weeks

       it's cool to be a miner again. taken us a long time to get
       there. to be in mining: to be in the news every day.

i drove up to see your mother.

       the big issues: lumber, copper, food, asia.

her friends and colleagues threw a baby shower for you, it was
monday morning. i was trying to get back to san diego in time for
class, the car broke down, the transmission went crazy, i had to
turn around. it was president's day, i couldn't find a single available
mechanic in davis.

       lumber producers are not only selling to internal
       markets anymore.

finally: a vietnamese family running a body shop outside of west
sacramento, it would take them at least two days to fix the car.

interesting global trend: the united states is no longer
setting prices.

the oldest son

there were two, and a daughter

was about 7, he found one of my stickers in the car.

yet the united states economy is stronger than what
you see on cnn, fox, and those places.

i told him he could have it, that it glowed in the dark, i don't think he
believed me. his sister kept trying to snatch the sticker, his younger
brother wouldn't stop staring at my t-shirt. i quickly scoured the car
for more stickers but couldn't find any. i found a ticket stub for
einstein on the beach, i smiled. a sense of rapture, perhaps this:
i could almost taste the music, where the end of your nostrils

meets the mouth of your throat. i wanted to cry. the clouds got heavy
i remembered the sticker. did i really want to cry?

and china isn't going anywhere, they have problems, yes
severe infrastructure problems, demographic problems
but they also have demand, a middle class that will
continue to demand things.

they charged me $387.43.

if communists want to stay in power, they have to give
the people economic hope, economic development.

second attempt: wednesday at 2:13pm. the roadways were fairly empty
the car was sluggish.

screaming for some water and some edible food

the eternal question: will mining companies make the right

decisions today for the future, or are we going to perpetuate this boom and bust ideology?

i couldn't stop thinking about the fact that you can now perceive light. it was sunny. every 10 miles or so, there would be groups of cows grazing peacefully, some close to the highway, others further away, resting under the shade of trees. i thought about those tv commercials: "happy cows come from california," now i can't stop thinking about mcdonalds maybe they own some of these pastures. will you like cows? i liked horses when i was really young, then i was afraid of them. i can't remember why, or when it happened either.

the chinese are incredibly disciplined buyers. they're buying on weakness on every single commodity.

all of a sudden, i was afraid of horses.

the world is drawing down on discoveries made in the past 40 years.

i don't want you to be afraid.

the average grade is dropping significantly in the big copper mines.

this world is made to instill fear.

and copper is the engine of the world, as copper goes the economy goes. or perhaps the other way around.

gas was almost $0.11 more expensive on the drive back, i didn't hit any traffic. i arrived in san diego before 11pm. i couldn't sleep, i started thinking about us, walking along the ocean beach pier with your mother. i would be carrying you, it would be sunny, but not too hot. you would have sunscreen, yes, sunscreen.

every mine in the world has problems. strikes. operational issues. governmental and environmental issues. every year we under-supply the world. what is keeping us in balance:

i want to show you the ocean

N.N.

where are the largest banks located?

where are the largest mines?

the uneven distribution of harm and benefits

copper mines

versus copper producers

always trace the money

"the linking that redeems all ugliness and vulgarity"[1]

1. *aisthesis*, jaques rancière

the sound of a baby crying should be the musical score of the *open pit*

in the andean cosmovision, the individual is
sociocentric, it is never conceived outside of the "we";
it does not disappear within the collective, rather, the
individual is always in conjunction with the rest, in
conjunction with the environment

how can you compare a cow with an apple?

the town of morococha is located in the province of yauli, in
the region of junín. it sits at 4540 meters above sea level, and
is 140 kilometers east of the city of lima. according to the
cerro de pasco archives, mining exploitation dates back to 1763.

hydroeconomic analysis: water and the economy

how can i live in your reality?

economic value per drop of water

y como yo digo siempre: aun muerta seguiré luchando

chinalco peru operates the toromocho mine site, located in morococha. through geological exploration, the firm's operators have found a reserve of 1,526 million metric tons of ore with an average grade of copper of 0.48 percent, an average grade of molybdenum of 0.02 percent, and silver of 6.88 grams per ton.

2014	2015	2016	2017	2018	bank	country
1	1	1	1	1	industrial & commercial bank of china	china
2	2	2	2	2	china construction bank corporation	china
3	3	3	3	3	agricultural bank of china	china
5	4	4	4	4	bank of china ltd.	china
8	5	5	5	5	mitsubishi ufj financial group	japan
4	6	7	7	7	hsbc holdings plc	uk
6	7	6	6	6	jpmorgan & chase co.	us
7	8	8	8	9	bnp pariba sa	france
9	9	9	9	8	bank of america corp.	us
12	10	10	10	10	crédit agricole group	france

2017	2018	mine	country	major owner/operator
1	1	escondida	chile	bhp
6	2	collahuasi	chile	anglo american/glencore
2	3	grasberg	indonesia	freeport mcmoran
5	4	cerro verde	perú	freeport mcmoran
10	5	el teniente	chile	codelco
3	6	morenci	usa	freeport mcmoran
7	7	antamina	perú	bhp/glencore
4	8	buenavista	méxico	southern copper
—	9	kghm polska	poland	kghm
8	10	las bambas	perú	mmg
18	19	toromocho	peru	chinalco

THE ORIGINAL INFRASTRUCTURE OF FUTURE BATTLEFIELDS

to maintain the fortress metabolic bodies in
constant motion amniotic fluid running through
your nostrils pulsations generating rhythm body
movement without structure leaching ponds laid
out in endless geometric patterns fractured
mountains a network of swollen arteries muscles
stretching the lack of phosphorous a maze
of embryonic tissue the original infrastructure
of future battlefields

let's try that again

instructions on how to maintain the fortress:

shake the necessary number of metabolic bodies

thrust in constant motion
count every single object arriving on time
through a nameless conveyor belt

be more specific, be more...

subversive?

be more effective

be more noneconomic

a network of swollen arteries
tailings pumping mercury into the reservoirs
an insatiable thirst for speed

know this:
or at least
to draw from

instructions

this world
beyond future
within capital(ism)

      how?

            he likes to stare at walls

          let's try that again

to extend the vortex metabolic bodies in tungsten
potions amniotic fluid running through our nostrils
rhythm generating pulsations body movement sit
down further teaching songs played out in endless
geometrical tatters the back is monstrous a trace
of tectonic fissures juridical in stark crutches

      how would this translate into spanish?

do you think i'm white?
a lot of (white) people in this country
tell me i'm not

things are so different
back home

hace un rato yo le decía
pregunta al uno
pregunta al otro
no te lleves de lo yo no más te digo
llévate del uno
lleváte del otro
y sacas tu conclusión

eso es

HOW IT WORKS

if i were more concerned with material accumulation
you would perhaps have more things
more toys, more books
we could even buy an apartment instead of rent one

do you feel like you have enough?

i don't read the newspapers
because they all have
ugly print

sometimes, i feel like i'm not being intelligent as a parent
and then i remember that view, when i was young, that hill
on the horizon. you could see it clearly from the country club
near our house. how different it looked at night:
glowing embers lined up in endless geometrical patterns

and during the day: dirt roads, no sewage, trash, esteras
for you, for us to have more things
places like this need to exist

i think that's how it works

THE WORLD IS WAITING IN LINE AT TARGET

imagine us in the car sunny day windows down

driving to the beach 88.3 driving and all those cars next to us driving
always in movement the highway is always full because the more
lanes we build the more cars are attracted to the smell of concrete
and white arrows painted over seemingly endless black surfaces:

the original infrastructure of future battlefields

imagine thousands of small highways running inside of you

all those cars driving somewhere taking something someone like us
perhaps to the beach with your mother so we would have the cooler
and the tent the umbrellas and the surfboards imagine all those cars
going somewhere taking something driving someone imagine all that
movement all that continuous movement the displacement dislocation
bodies inside metal vehicles on black surfaces running

imagine thousands of small really really small

a huge conveyor belt a network of swollen arteries imagine an open pit
an open wound the skin rupturing imagine your leg imagine your arm

imagine my leg imagine my arm

a big bag of tendons and ligaments necrotic tissue a bundle of nerve
tissue imagine bags of plastic inside your stomach lining your
intestines and climbing up your esophagus through the larynx
the lack of oxygen

imagine these huge pond type structures with plastic geothermal
liners stretching across the mountains dissecting the mountains
becoming the new mountain the only landscape leaching ponds laid
out in endless geometrical patterns

imagine every single muscle every fiber every synapse every neuron
needed for you to type with your right index finger:

m. m. m.

the letter m

imagine thousands of small highways pulsating inside of you

corazón corazón mal herido

imagine it never stopping

seré tu héroe de amor

thousands of small highways and the cars and the people and the things
and the places they want to take those things to because that's what we
do we go places with things and we use metal vehicles that travel on
seemingly endless black surfaces just imagine all of this happening all
the time all the time happening all the time always

this highway

there's no outside

this open pit

this wound this rupture this crevice inside body this highway all the time
always

what i'm trying to say miqel is:

just imagine thousands of small highways always running inside of you

imagine everything that's needed for this to happen

all the time

always

now imagine an open pit a large open pit in the middle of a valley
surrounded by fractured mountains

i think that's how it works

we have that pit

we keep running: faster faster faster

birds die and their stomachs are filled with plastic

whales die and their stomachs are filled with plastic

the.US economy gets a billion-dollar daily shot in its arm

imagine your arm

i'm thinking of mine

we have that pit

and we fill it with these things

we keep running faster always faster

now imagine us at the beach, imagine it being sunny again but not
too hot, imagine the sky punctuated by a few curious clouds, your
mother would be smiling, she's beautiful when she smiles
it's still happening

i don't know what it is

i'm not sure what to do about it either

but i know it's happening, all the time, always, relentless

we have that pit, it's open, really open

and things are exploding and people breaking and burning and dying

and we're distracted

because we love the sand
the salt in the water
the cool air

este hospital me está matando
no sé porque me tienen aquí
la morfina me está matando lento
quiero estar con mis hijos
alguien nos tiene que escuchar

1 ml. morphine hydrochloride
10 mg / ml
injectable solution
intrathecal, epidural
s.c., i.m. o e.v.
r.s. n-ng-1393
digemid

in 2012 the peruvian government and the chinese mining company chinalco began the relocation of the residents of morococha to the town of nueva morococha (carhuacoto), located 7 kilometers to the east. several families resisted at first, and there were protests. the peruvian government declared a state of emergency in morococha in 2013, which allowed it to close down the schools and health centers, leaving the families resisting the relocation process with very few choices.

no tenemos suficiente dinero para tener justicia

lunch in morococha, first day (august 2014)

como alcalde tenía que luchar por su pueblo
pero, muchas veces que el dinero puede
y humillas a los demás
eso es lo que está pasando

antes estábamos mejor que ahora

11° 36' 40.72" S
76° 8' 21.25" W

we were unconventional
from the beginning
your mother and i

weren't together, as a couple

you came unexpected
and we loved you
since before you were born

      la oficina del alcalde es una mina

the people of morococha are indigenous, andean, mestizo. the peruvian government would've never done this in the predominantly white districts of miraflores and san isidro, which are only 155 kilometers away, in the city of lima.

      the uneven distribution of harm and benefits

YOUR COMPUTER IS KILLING MOROCOCHA

instructions:

the actant that's not one of the actants that forms part of the body of the open pit should read as background noise, and at a lower volume, running each sentence against the next, (although not necessarily fast). the text is also meant to be read as a closed loop: the actant returns to the beginning when reaching the end. the actant that's not one of the actants that forms part of the body of the open pit should stop reading and remain silent whenever the parent is reading. the body of the open pit should read somewhat slowly, making an effort to pronounce each word as clearly as possible. both capital and the actant that's not one of the actants that forms part of the body of the open pit begin reading at the same time.

*

component
monitor
phosphorescent coating
transition
metals

element
compound
zinc sulfide
silver chlorine
europium
copper
yitrium silicate

mineral
source
sulfur and zincite
halite
cuprite and gold
flourite
pyrope
biotite
talc

our fathers went to the same school together. our grandparents knew each other well. they frequented the same country club, although the differences were quite noticeable.

crt glass

lead
iron and silicon

galena and quartz

████████ and i went to the same school our fathers did: an all-boys catholic school
with the same group of students from kindergarten to senior year in high school.

plastic
case keyboard
thermo-polypropylene
additive
white pigment
carbon titanium
phosphorus
phosphate
ammonium

gypsum
rutile

limenite
apetite
wavellite

governed first by nuns, then priests, then teachers. you will probably not go to this school miqel. you will probably not hang out with ██████████'s son or daughter.

liquid crystal
display
thin film
transistors

lead
indium
tin
oxide

daddy how come you're never around?
i miss you

anglesite

                    quartz
                    sphalerite

you will probably not enter tonka heaven. our fathers were not quite friends; they respected each other,
but from a certain distance.

              metal case

                              iron

          magnetite
          limonite

the two families: ████████ y villarán. now they run the largest gold mine in latin america. your grandaunt
was the first elected woman mayor in the history of lima.

              printed circuit
              boards
              silicon chips

silver
aluminum
arsenic

malachite
boronite
azurite

i live in san diego, california, and write about extractivism on a computer made primarily from minerals. you'll be one-year old next week

79 mine/ banner district/ near hayden/ gila county/ arizona

machen quarry/ near caerphilly

east java/ indonesia near the kawah ijen volcano

frongoch mine/ devil's bridge/ ceredigion

sterling mine/ ogdensburg/ sterling hill/ sussex county/ new jersey

the darling ranges of western australia/ the first mine pit was at the jarrahdale site now known as langford park

the huntly mine is located near dwellingup and was established in early 1976

the mandla district of madhya pradesh / located 466 km south-east of bhopal

the hilton mine in westmorland
the beaumont (allenheads) and saint peters mines in northumberland

the moretown talc mine / located just over the line into fayston / this talc mine was
not the more famous mine operated by eastern magnesia talc / located in north
moretown up near the winooski river

merkers mine/ thuringia / germany

intrepid potash east mine / carlsbad potash district / new mexico

morenci / greenlee county / arizona

winsford rock salt mine is britain's oldest working mine / it lies almost 200m under
the cheshire countryside
bingham canyon / salt lake city / utah

broken hill / yancowinna county / new south wales / australia escondida is a copper mine in the atacama desert / located in the antofagasta region of chile

chingola / about 100km northeast of ndola / is where konkola copper mine / zambia's largest mine / and nchanga / its only open pit mine (both owned by london-listed vedanta resources) are located

parys mountain mines / amlwch / isle of anglesey / wales / the united kingdom

tsumeb mine / otavi-bergland district / oshikoto / namibia

mission complex / pima county / arizona

monteponi mine / monteponi / sardinia / italy

I LIKE TO STARE AT WALLS

you were born in davis
in a small inflatable pool
in april

during those first weeks, you would often wake up crying
in the middle of the night. without really knowing how
i would pick you up from the crib, and hold you against
my chest, until you calmed down
and fell asleep again

i liked staying like this for a while
staring at the darkness
that would become the wall

here comes the river
over the flames

do i have the right to tell the story of morococha?

antes estábamos mejor
cuando teníamos minería a socavón
chinalco es un cáncer
este pueblo debería de estar pujante
alguien tiene que contar nuestra historia
las primeras palabras de mi hijo:
ollanta traidor

the psychological impact of the forceful relocation
process on the children of morococha

are we making history
or are we simply running
to an already scheduled appointment?[1]

1. dagwami yimer

sendero luminoso stole dynamite sticks from the mines

who does the earth think they are?

the earth is alive miqel
and screaming

can you hear them?

these songs are a representation of the space we traveled and the time we shared, and at some point miqel, when i was living in san diego, and driving up to davis to see you on the weekends, this space/time was our only home, our first refuge, the one place we could be together on our own terms, and where no one else would bother us; this was our first home, on the road, driving

the lyrics
a cartography of the territories
the imaginaries we navigated and inhabited
this was our first home
in the car
in the music
on an endless california highway

and a trace of the ubiquitous nature
of 21st century capitalism
capable of penetrating even the most intimate spaces
the songs are always on shuffle = algorithm

los trabajadores de chinalco están prohibidos consumir lo que acá vendemos

(flight instructions)

ONE DAY IN THE LIFE OF THE SOCIAL ROCK

the rock wakes up and smiles / looks around

either from siberia
or from europe
or from east asia or africa

by crossing beringia
the solutrean hypothesis
pedro furada

the rock smiles / looks around / plays with pen

kotosh
3000 to 1800 BCE

olmeca
1400 to 400 BCE

chavín
900 to 250 BCE

maya
2000 BCE to 1600 CE

the rock smiles / looks around / plays with pen / twirls
pen on table

mochica
100 to 800 CE

tolteca
800 to 1000 CE

huanca
1000 to 1460

mexicas
1428 to 1519

incas
1438 to 1533

the rock doesn't really smile / looks around confused / kind of plays
with pen / twirls pen on table / taps pen gently on table

spanish colonial period
1500s–1820s

spanish colonial period
1500s–1820s

independence
perú: july 28, 1821

independence
méxico: september 27, 1821

        the rock doesn't really smile / looks around confused and angry /
        kind of plays with pen / kind of twirls pen on table / taps pen on
        table more insistently

delfina godoy y godoy
1859–1884
could argue her way out of anything

        his grandmother's great grandfather (father's side)

jesús gonzález ortega
1822–1891
governor of zacatecas, general
fought next to benito juárez

        his grandfather's great granduncle (mother's side)

the rock doesn't smile at all/ looks around in anger / doesn't play
with pen / doesn't twirl pen on table / bangs pen on table more
insistently / harder and harder

district of morococha
founded in 1907
province of yauli

mexican revolution
1910–1929

either you pay with your life

although the country was in a state of turmoil
until the end of the 1930s

or you pay dues and homage

1928–cerro de pasco corporation
sinks morococha lagoon
(more than 30 workers dead)

compensation: 50 soles per family

the rock doesn't smile at all/ looks around in anger / does not play
with pen / does not twirl pen on table / bangs pen on table violently /
harder and harder / louder and louder

centromin corporation
state owned
1976

amelia ramona magdaleno penilla
1917–1979
"kidnapped" for love as a teenager
went hungry for weeks with her infant son and daughter

his grandmother (mother's side)
she died the year he was born

may 17, 1980
shining path's first act of war

they used to steal dynamite sticks
from the mines

the rock doesn't smile / looks around in anger / does not play with
pen / does not twirl pen on table / bangs pen on table violently /
harder and harder / louder and louder / almost as if in a trance

minera copper sa takes over toromocho operation
2004

i graduated from sfsu
and returned to lima
2005

president alan garcía
2006–2011
president hu jin-tao
2002–2012

free trade agreement
perú and china
2008

rosalía lavalle de morales macedo
founded el hogar de la madre
1903–1977

                              his grandmother's aunt (father's side)

                    the rock doesn't smile / looks around in anger / does not play with
                    pen / does not twirl pen on table / bangs pen on table violently /
                    harder and harder / louder and louder / almost as if in a trance /
                    pen on table

        chinalco and the peruvian government
        shut down schools, health centers, businesses
        morococha
        2012

you were born in davis, california
in a beautiful hospital, in a pool
miqel villarán garcía
2013

                              they agreed on his name during the 10th hour of labor

200 families still in morococha
defying chinalco and the peruvian government
2014

i present the *open pit*
as my qualifying examination materials
ucsc, 2017

        the rock doesn't smile / looks around in confusion and sadness /
        looks at pen on table

    how can we weaponize his privilege?
    how can we weaponize his privilege?

jose antonio villarán gonzález-ortega

        the rock looks at pen on table
        shakes head from side to side:

        all they care about

their own little stories
all they care about

their
own
little
stories

N.N.

i met someone miqel
her name is ▮▮▮▮▮▮
(i like her a lot)

how does one start at the beginning?
if things happen before they actually happen[1]

i'm not sure what i expected miqel, that maybe the people still living in morococha and resisting the peruvian government and the chinalco mining company, that maybe the gathering of efforts from that position would be less complicated?

carlos r. pflucker (1830), establishes facilities to refine copper: la hacienda mineral pflucker in morococha

1. *the hour of the star*, clarice lispector

i'm not sure what to make of the plurality of voices within the people still living in morococha,
i'm not sure how to understand it, or how to articulate it

census 1876:
500 people

antonio raimondi spent a month at the hacienda
pflucker in 1861 and painted a series of now famous
water paintings

are these process notes here
because he doesn't trust readers
or because he trusts them completely?

i can't believe
you can now conjugate verbs
use pronouns

perhaps both

                    mío

        tuyo

                        nosotros

                        nosotres

i want to live well mijo
i want us to live well

> "*buen vivir* is not a fixed value proposition; rather, it is perma-
> nently evolving. that said, certain building blocks facilitate the
> construction of *buen vivir*, including knowledge, ethical and
> spiritual codes of conduct that define how to relate with the envi-
> ronment, and human values and visions of the future. *buen vivir*
> or *sumak kawsay* is key to the philosophy of life in indigenous
> societies"[1]

1. "*buen vivir*: an alternative perspective from the peoples of the global south to the crisis of capitalist modernity"; alberto
acosta, mateo martínez abarca.

PUBLIC HEALTH STATEMENT OR ███████████ IS IN THE ALMENARA HOSPITAL

instructions:

the people can imagine reading from a hospital bed on a hot muggy day without air conditioning and a stream of visitors swarming the cramped shared and poorly sterilized spaces. the actant that's not one of the actants that forms part of the body of the open pit should read as background noise, and at a lower volume, running each sentence against the next, (although not necessarily fast). the text is also meant to be read as a closed loop, the actant returns to the beginning when reaching the end. both the people and the actant that's not one of the actants that forms part of the body of the open pit begin reading at the same time.

*

the use of company or product name(s) is for identification only and does not imply endorsement by the agency for toxic substances and disease registry

the use of company or product name(s) is for identification only and does not imply endorsement by the agency for toxic substances and disease registry

the use of company or product name(s) is for identification only and does not imply endorsement by the agency for toxic substances and disease registry

use of company product name(s) identification only does not imply endorsement agency toxic substances disease registry

use company or product identification does not endorsement the agency toxic disease registry

use company name identification endorsement agency toxic registry

use name identification agency toxic disease registry

use name agency toxic registry

name agency toxic
use name

registry

toxic registry

use

use

the use of company or product name(s) is for identification only and does not imply endorsement by the agency for toxic substances and disease registry

the use of company or product name(s) is for identification only and does not imply endorsement by the agency for toxic substances and disease registry

the use of company or product name(s) is for identification only and does not imply endorsement by the agency for toxic substances and disease registry

the use of product name(s) identification only does not imply endorsement agency toxic substances disease registry

use or product identification does not endorsement imply the agency toxic disease registry

use company name identification endorsement agency toxic registry

use name identification agency toxic disease registry

use name agency toxic registry

use name agency disease

agency disease name
use name registry

disease

use

use

por indignación y de tanto miedo
porque era demasiado abuso
mi distrito estaba lleno de policías
ya no se podía caminar
y no habían respuestas para darles a nuestros hijos

what is copper?
what is gold?
what is mercury?

what is uranium?
what is lead?

air

                water

sediment and soil

                other media

me acuerdo que llamaron a una reunión
y me paré ante las autoridades y le dije
ya basta de abuso
esto no puedo seguir

what happens to copper when it enters the environment?
what happens to gold when it enters the environment?
what happens to mercury when it enters the environment?
what happens to uranium when it enters the environment?
what happens to lead when it enters the environment?

pharmacokinetic mechanisms

mechanisms of toxicity

animal to human extrapolations

toxicokinetics

other routes of exposure

porque no somos delincuentes
no somos rateros
no hemos violado a nadie
ni mucho menos hemos matado
hagamos fuerza
alguien nos tiene que oír
alguien tiene que saber

how might we be exposed to copper?
how might we be exposed to gold?

how might we be exposed to mercury?
how might we be exposed to uranium?
how might we be exposed to lead?

biomarkers used to identify exposure to copper

biomarkers used to quantify exposure to gold

biomarkers used to identify exposure to mercury

biomarkers used to quantify exposure to uranium

biomarkers used to characterize exposure to arsenic

y a las doce de la noche estábamos partiendo a lima
con nuestros niños
a reclamar
y que nos escuchen

how can copper enter and leave our body?
how can gold enter and leave our body?
how can mercury enter and leave our body?
how can uranium enter and leave our body?
how can lead enter and leave our body?

reducing peak absorption following exposure

reducing body burden

interfering with the mechanism of action for toxic effects

reducing body burden

other routes of exposure

y gracias el haber venido a lima
lo único, no logramos mucho
pero logramos que nuestra zona deje de ser militarizada

i got a bone to pick

how can copper affect my health?
how can gold affect my health?
how can mercury affect my health?
how can uranium affect my health?
how can lead affect my health?

air

water

soil

environmental fate

y desde que me metí a la lucha
he sufrido mucho porque
no es fácil ser mujer y encabezar una marcha
porque, me secuestraron a mi
unos policías luego me asaltaron

how can copper affect children?
how can gold affect children?
how can mercury affect children?
how can uranium affect children?
how can lead affect children?

production

import/export

use

disposal

y mi hijo es, nació allí
por eso la defiendo
por tanta injusticia
tanto miedo
me volví rebelde
y es por eso que lucho

how can families reduce the risk of exposure to copper?
how can families reduce the risk of exposure to gold?
how can families reduce the risk of exposure to mercury?
how can families reduce the risk of exposure to uranium?
how can families reduce the risk of exposure to lead?

transport and partitioning

transformation and degradation

identification of data needs

elimination and excretion

adequacy of the database

más antes no entendía yo tampoco porque luchar
pero cuando esto llegó a mi pueblo
entendí mucho

entendí mucho y le eché ganas a luchar
me metí con todo a esta lucha

is there a test to determine if we have been exposed to copper?
is there a test to determine if we have been exposed to gold?
is there a test to determine if we have been exposed to mercury?
is there a test to determine if we have been exposed to uranium?
is there a test to determine if we have been exposed to lead?

absorption

genotoxicity

oral exposure

dermal exposure

other routes of exposure

y como yo digo siempre
aún muerta seguiré luchando

aún muerta
seguiré luchando

your favorite word is poto
poroto
cara de choclo

toner in relation to hesitancy
to be in the wandering
looking for a new vocabulary
to document the process

la clave está
en el traspaso
entre peru copper
y la chinalco,
allí está

(la venta de morococha se hizo en las islas caimán)

does the story store stuff for us?

it's also important to tell a story

"the function of poetry has changed so much—
doesn't tell stories, instruct, is not recited as rite,
does not distill the people's wisdom or even prophesy much.
what does it do then?"[1]

1. *disobedience*, alice notley

AN IMAGINARY CONVERSATION WITH ███████████

a journalist from one of the most prestigious newspapers in perú,
that covered news related to morococha as early as 2008

q. what was it about the story of morococha that caught your attention?

a.

q. did you ever imagine things would end up like this?

a.

q. what was the response from your editors and colleagues when you insisted in covering the news related to the people of morococha, when most of the country only cared about receiving the mining royalties from the toromocho project?

a.

q. did you get in trouble for helping ███████████ pass as one of your cameramen so that he could enter congress and make a statement in front of the whole assembly?

a.

q. i met ████████ a couple of years ago, through a friend in common. we're still in contact, he's helping me out with this project. he's now living in nueva morococha, did you know that?

a.

q. did you ever feel threatened by representatives from the peruvian government or the chinalco mining company?

a.

q. how do you feel at 4,540 meters above sea level?

a.

q. what do you think is going to happen to old morococha?

a.

q. and the people still living there?

a.

q. after my first trip to morococha in 2014, i felt completely defeated and confused, i couldn't shake that feeling, even now. did you ever feel disheartened, discouraged, depleted, when covering the news related to morococha and the toromocho mining project?

a.

q. i often think about you, although i can't really picture you. what do you think i should do with all this work/research? do you think i have a right to talk about morococha? do i have a right to tell their story?

a.

q. after all these years (more than 6 at this point), after talking to different people, after reading all those books, i'm actually more confused, and i feel like i understand less, in terms of what to do about this situation, about what to do in towns like morococha, how to reconcile the plurality of voices, what to do about the role of extractivism, about our relation to the earth (now i'm thinking of my son). after all these years, how do you feel?

a.

q. and what do you think can be done about it?

a.

q. is it worth fighting then?

a.

q. one of the women i talked to in relation to this project, said this to me: *"even dead i'll keep fighting"*. what would you say to the president of the chinalco mining company?

a.

q. and to the president of perú?

a.

q. and if you could send a message to the people of morococha, what would it be?

a.

my analyst told me
i'm taking to therapy
like a duck in water

what the fuck does that mean?

"when one lives in a world that is collapsing,
constructing a book perhaps may be one of the few
survival tactics"[1]

how to combine:

the story of morococha
the story of my family

1. lumpérica, diamela eltit

his mom is from the north
his dad is from the south
he's somewhere in between

for a little bit of fame today
for a name in the usa

"seen geographically and understood politically, the
process of extraction is a profound and deep-rooted
ideology of self-entitlement"[1]

1. *extraction empire*, ed. pierre bolanger

and your mom is together with ▮▮▮ and i'm with ▮▮▮▮▮ and we all love you and we're all one big family kind of and i miss you so much sometimes and it makes me sad to live so far away from you and this sadness somehow becomes guilt i feel guilty guilty for not being there with you i feel guilty and i feel sad that things ended up like this because ▮▮▮ has leukemia and needs to stay in philadelphia for his treatment his insurance and i know you like it there which makes me happy and at the same time i feel sad because i'm not there with you i'm not there with you not there and it doesn't matter that it's not my fault or because of something i did the fact is i'm not there with you and all this love all this love i have for you all this love all this love i have for you somehow gets twisted and i feel guilty twisted because i want to be there with you i want i want to be there with you i want i want to be there with you and i'm not

i want to be there with you and i'm not
i want i want to be there with you
and i'm not

A QUESTION OF INDEBTEDNESS

i can feel the debt
pulsating through my body
(cada centavo que debo)
i can feel the different interest rates
calculating themselves
with every step i take

i wonder if my dissertation committee wants me to write like this
so direct and obvious and devoid of artifice

and i don't know what i'm doing here but i'm scared because i can feel the debt pulsating through my body

i can feel the music arriving from somewhere

everything is free now
that's what they say

my son will be six years old next week and i hate the fact that i live so far away from him i hate the fact that the university forces me to compete and professionalize compete and professionalize compete and professionalize and i don't think that's what i want to do with my writing the university is fucked up right now i can feel the debt pulsating through my body the different interest rates each loan calculating itself with every word i write i write in the university not of the university and still in the university and i think fred moten's work is necessary i'm also suspicious of his complicity

i'm suspicious of my own complicity all of us in the university complicit and the millions of students incurring debt everyday billions and trillions of dollars and do you really want to know how it feels at 4,540 meters above sea level?

i'm here, in san francisco

sieged by all this tech money and complaining about the public university in the united states while the people of morococha get screwed by the peruvian government and the chinalco mining company and our indifference

i feel compelled
i feel obliged
their story
i can feel the debt pulsating through my body
it works
in mysterious ways

N.N.

you're going to have a sister miqel
ramona
like abuelita's mom
ramona
her name is ramona

███████ and i so are happy

instructions:

for 3 actants: capital starts reading first. three seconds later, people starts reading, government starts reading three seconds after people. the actants must stop and wait for three seconds after reading two lines. the actants can also stop for three seconds after reading one line but cannot read three lines in a row without stopping. the thing is done after the actants read every single line.

for 24 actants: the actants are divided into groups of three; capital, people, government, each group is assigned one of the 8 pages. the actants must stop and wait for three seconds after reading two lines, the actants can also stop for three seconds after reading one line, but cannot read three lines in a row without stopping. capital from the first page starts reading first, three seconds later, the people starts reading, government starts reading three seconds after people. capital from the second page starts reading three seconds after people from the first page starts reading. the actants continue this pattern until the 8 pages are done.

i don't want your one stop shops or virtual windows
i don't want your your your massive anti-mining protests
i don't want your windfall profits taxes or previous consultations
i don't want your villages obssttructing our investment plans
i don't want your llamas or vicuñas your alpacas your trout
i don't want your sacred mountain tops or pristine water basins
i don't want your environmental impact assessmentsss

i don't want your 5g networks or 2-hour shipping delivery
i don't want your i don't want your your supreme decrees
i don't wwant your leaching ponds near mmy villages
i don't want your i don't want your i don't want your your
i don't want your top regional ranking your development index
i don't want your children thinking they're better than our children
i don't want your social programs to run out of federal funding

i don't want your your massive anti-mining protests
i don't wwant your your antiquated worlddviews
i ddon't want your private cclubs in our beeaches
i don't want your municipal stadiums in your small villages
i don't want your i don't wwant your want i don't wwwant
i don't want your old-money families running the country
i don't want your children growing-up without opportunities

i want mmmy 5g network my 2-hour shipping delivery
i want my streamlined processes my vertical accountability
i want my exclusive beach resorts my security guards
i want my trips to miami new york london the caribbean
i want my private schools with their international programs
i want my i want my i want my want my mmy mmy my
i want my tax exemptions mmmy preferential options

i want my schools in quechua aymara shipibo aguaruna
i want mmy sacred mountain tops our forests our lakes
i wwant woh work if i work i can educate mmy children
i want mmmy healthcare i want mmy mmy social sservices
i want my mayor mmy regional rehreh representatives
i want my ssshhade grown ccofffee in international markets
i want my mmy i wwant mmy i want our our i want our

i wwant my mmy ssocial programs mmy sssubsiddies
i want mmy schools in ssppanish in english cchinnese
i want ecoefficiency measures mmy impact assessments
i wwant mmmy i wwwant mmy i want my i want my i
i want my exports arriving to the wworld's largest ports
i want mmy my bbbillions of ddollars in minning taxes
i want my top regional ranking mmmy development index

i don't want my remediation plans my environmental liabilities
i ddon't wwant mmy my mmmy ddd ddon't want dddd don't
i don't wwwant my windfall profits taxes or previous consultation
i don't want mmmy books my private schools in quechua or aymara
i don't want my feasibility studies rejected yourrrr jester politicians
i don't wwwant i don't wwaaannt wwaaant want my wwawant my
i don't want my private beach clubs invaded the whole countryside

i don't want mmy i don't wwant my mmy dddon't wwant mmy
i don't want mmy books my schools only in spanish english chinese
i don't wwant my villages mmy villages sieged bbby the police
i don't want our mountains our rivers our water basins polluted
i don't want mmmy indigenous languages ridiculed in congresss
i dddon't want my dddon't want mmy wawawant mmmmy
i don't wwwant my crops ttoo ttoo run ouut of wwwater

who do i make checks payable to?

i don't wwant my social programs to run out of funding
i dddon't want mmy i don't wwwawant my don't www
i don't wwant my taxes ttto scare away investments
i don't want mmmy i ddon't wwwant i ddd ddd don't
i don't want my previous consultation sscare investments
i don't wwwant my environmental impact assessments to ssscare away
foreign invvvestments i don't wwant mmy

i want yyyour i wwwaant waaaaant your i want yyyour
i want your books your schools in spanish in english chinese
i wwwwant your your your natural ree ree resources yyour
i want yyyour ree ree resssentment to fffinally enndd
i wwant your llllaws to mmean ssommesomething i want
i wwwant yyyyour sseats in cccon ccconngress i i i
i i wwant your children readddy new gglobal oordder

i wwant your preevious cconsultation ttto meann something
i want your bbooks your sschools also in quechua shipibo aymara
i wwwant your ccontacts your mmmoney yyyour ppowwer
i want yyyour chchillddren to pplay with mmy chchilddrenn
i wwwant your ssshopping malls yyour 5g nnnetwork
i want your ccountry clubs your pprivate beaches open public
i wwant your i wwwant i i i i want i wwwant i wwwant your

i wwant your schools in spanish ennglish quechua
i want yyour mmmyaami your nnew york your pparis
i wwwant yyyour i wwwant i want i wwwa wwwwa
i want yyour beacchh clubs open ttto the publicc
i want yyyyour i want yyyour i want yyyyour your
i want your rrresentment your rrrage to enddd
i wwwant yyour cccoffee in llargest tttrade ffairs

you ddon't want my sssttrategic plllans you ddon't wwant
you don't want mmmy clubs enjoyed bby real owwners
yyou don't wwant my schools engglish frenchch chinese
yyyyou dddon't want ddon't wwant dddon't wwant mmmy
you don't wwant my fffamily my traddditions my history
you don't want mmmy dddon't wwant mmmy ddddon't
yyyou don't wwwant wwwant want want don't wwant

you ddon't want my books in qquechua in aymara aguaruna
you don't wwant my llammmas my alpppacas my guinea pigs
yyou don't want don't wwant mmy don't wwwant mmmy
you ddon't want mmy daughters having same opportttunities
yyyou don't wwant to pressserve nnnatureture don't wwant
you dddon't wwwaant mmmy mmmy yyyou don't wwwant
you ddon't wwant my interconnectedness other sspeciess

yyou don't want mmy social programs nno funddding
you dddon't wwant my my mmy you ddon't wwant my
you don't wwant my schools ennnglish chchchinese
yyyou dddon't want mmmy tttaxes mmy ttaxxxs
you don't wwant my pppreevvious consssulttation
youuu dddon't wwant ddon't want yyou yyou yyyou
ddon't wwant yyou dddon't wwant yyou ddon't want

yyou wwant your yyour ssschools your ssschools you wwwant
you want yyyyour yyyyour yyou wwant yyyyour pppolice
yyyou wwwant yyyyour yyyyyyour yyyyyyour your yyyyou
wwwwant yyyyyyour yyyyour awwway invvvestmmments
yyou wwwannt yyour childddren yyyour rrrressentffful
you wwwant yyyyour yyyou wwwawwant yyyyour yyyou
wwant yyyour ppovvverty eraddicccationnn yyou wwwant

yyou wwa wwant yyour ppprivvate ssschools yyyou yyyou
wwant yyour bbbeach ccclubbs yyyou wwwwant yyour
yyyyou wwwant yyour yyyou yyyyou wwant wwwannt
yyyou want wwwant yyour yyyyyou wwant yyyour yyou
wwant yyyour chchch yyou wwant yyour chchiilddren
yyyou wwant yyyyour yyyou wwwant yyyyour yyyou
yyyou wwant yyyour yyyou wwaant yyyou wwwant

yyou want yyour ssschools ennnglishh ffffrench chch
yyyou want yyyyour bbeachch cclubbbs yyyouu yyou
wwwwant yyyour pppreevvious ccconsssultationn
yyyour ennvvironmenntal impact assessmmments
yyyou wwwwant yyyour yyyou wwwant yyyyour
yyyou wwant yy your chchildren no oppportttunities
yyou want yyyour ttttaxes yyyour ttttaxes yyou wwant

yyou ddon't wwant yyour yyour books inn ennnglish
yyyou don't wwwant yyour mmunicipal ssstadiums
yyou don't want your social programs out of funding
you ddon't wwant yyour yyour mmillions in ttaxes
you don't want your yyyou ddon't want your you
you ddon't wwwant yyour your sseats in ccongress
you don't want your children growing modern country

you don't want your ssschols in kwecha shipibo aguaruna
you ddon't want your laws your laws to actually work
you don't want cclubs your beaches open to the public
yyou don't wwwant your you don't wwant your you
you ddon't wwant your envvironmental liabilities
you don't want your old-money families sharing power
you don't want yyour children thinking of uss equals

you don't wwant your social programs nno funding
yyou don't want your schools in spanish english chch
you don't want yyour your mmunicipal stadiumss
you don't wwant your beach clubs open the public
yyou don't want you're your yyou don't wwant your
you ddon't want your your remmediation ppplans
you don't want yyour children growing up opportunities

you want my my private clubs my beaches you wwant mmy
yyou want my millions of ddollars in taxes for social programs
you want mmy schools my shopping malls my golf courses
you want my vacations my miami my new york my caribbean
you wwant my ttax exemptions mmy prefferential options
you want mmy families my traddditions mmy ccontacts
yyou wwant my investments mmy sstrategic visionn

you want my shade grown mmy women grown my altitude my
yyou want our sacred mmountain tops our lakes our rivers
you wwant my llamas my vicuñas you want mmy trout
you want mmy seats you want all of my sseats in congress
yyou want my children to alwways be yyour subbaltern
you want my prevvious consultation my social pprograms
you want my mmunicipal stadiums my medical centers

you wwant my millions of ddollars in taxes
you want my schools in kwecha shipibo aguaruna
yyou want my ccconcessions my legal loopholes
yyou wwant my my ecoeffficiency measures
you want my ports my my preferential tariffs
you want my supreme decrees my congress
you want my highways my hospitals my stadiums

N.N.

you call me pami sometimes
papi-mami
i love it

                how can these two places
                exist in the same world?

     morococha: forceful relocation process, residents fighting for rights, pollution
     lack of opportunities

        whole foods on ocean avenue in san francisco: 1-hour food delivery
        organic avocados for $3.99 each

no hay que tener miedo vecinos
no hay que temerle a la empresa chinalco

                        usa el amor
                  usa el amor como un puente

it's all coming together miqel
your sister ramona is growing strong
██████ and i are starting to buy her things

we're going to use your first stroller
do you remember it?

it is strong
and you are tough

it's all coming together miqel
i'm making progress on my dissertation
my therapy is going well
i feel less anxious

it's all coming together mijo
it's all coming together

89

10 POTENTIAL SCENARIOS FOR ANY GIVEN CONDITIONS

[instructions: there's usually always an exception to the rule]

*

francisco barrick pizarro a bull with no horns

their own little stories 15 more dead guinea pigs

an endless conveyor belt new windfall profits taxes

200 families still living in 8,200 tons of copper (2015)

11° 36' 40.72" s

walls without staring positions

the capacity to refuse

an open pit torn from within

nintendo sounding breathers

walls filled with minerals

5 fake supreme decrees

a bigger football stadium

kayllam kayllam kayllam

4,540 meters above sea level

skarns mantles and veins

an unfinished phd thesis

4540 METERS

i talk to the people
and study and visit the sites
and listen to the experts
and i understand less
and less
about what to do
extractivism

i understand less
about what to do
in a town like morococha

i feel more knowledgeable on the subject
and at the same time
more confused and discouraged

because in the end, does it actually matter all that much? things keep moving at the same hectic pace, lebron james didn't make the playoffs for the first time since he was like 13 and there will be a new iphone coming out in a few weeks, as well as another marvel superhero movie. the people of morococha, the town of morococha, are part of this transaction, some of us just don't quite understand the underlying mechanisms, or we pretend to ignore them, because in the end, do you really want to know how it feels at 4,540 meters above sea level?

do you really?

N.N.

"the re-encounter with nature is another of the priority points on the agenda, and this means doing away with models and practices centered on the exploitation and appropriation of nature"[1]

"who's playing papi?"

liverpool versus arsenal
who do you want to win?

"both papi, both"

francisco barrick pizarro

1. "extractivism and neo-extractivism: two sides of the same curse"; alberto acosta

i walk through the streets of nueva morococha

la voz del pueblo es la voz de dios

extractive violence is also racial violence

i think i might be the only white person around

ya sabemos ya quienes son los culpables

perpetrated against the indigenous people
against the black and brown people
against the not-wealthy people of this world

hasta los policías de acá, defienden a la empresa

N.N.

things got fucked miqel
really fucked
there's something wrong
with ramona's brain
i can't believing this is happening
i can't believe this is real .

i

once again, the voices, lost, the people, morococha, lost, their own words, once again, become invisible, like a specter that gravitates in the depths, once again, the voices, lost, a loss, an absence, i carry inside, morococha, once again, it's not a surprise, although it's still surprising, the persistence of the loss, the inability of an attempt to recover, once again, we're back at the point of departure

what does it mean to lose?

i was, am there, listening, in the break, the recordings lost, the digital notes, yet their voices live inside of me, and they come out to sing, as i close my eyes, the clouds get heavy, and i can't stop crying, once again, we're back at the point of departure

ii

sarita's *salchipapas* joint on main street, which is called main and is also the main street in town, ███'s hostel, ███'s friend, where i stayed during my last visit, and which had an internet *cabina* where a handful of teens would gather in the evenings to play call of duty. la olla de barro, where i would eat breakfast every day and watch all the miners chat it up and get ready for work, before loading up their decked-out suvs, the candlelight vigil to raise awareness about the next strike, the persistent, biting dryness in the air, the coldness that seeps deep into your bones, the perpetual *soroche* headache that bullied me every night because of my damn coastal blood, those 4 kids playing on the street next to the municipality, oblivious to the public hearing taking place inside, the way in which the mountains stretch abruptly towards the sky, as if they were trying to embrace the clouds, or perhaps trying to escape from the rotten smell of the tailings' deposits

this urgency to write, to remember everything, because the recordings are lost, once again, the notes are lost, once again, the phone's screen cracked, the information inaccessible, the voices of the people lost, trapped within that disabled device

iii

this urgency, to remember the river's murmuring, which wouldn't stop singing, the calmness ██████████ conveyed, and his nineties looking sunglasses, in that quarry
20 kilometers inwards from morococha, that is now his

this urgency to write, to not forget anything, because the recordings, lost, and the digital notes, the phone, the screen smashed, the device, disabled

i feel this urgency, this urgency, i feel like i'm going to forget something, because i'm so sad, because my daughter ramona died four weeks ago, during her 6th month in cristina's womb, and my older brother kiko died last week, probably from a heart attack or a stroke, while he was playing football in vietnam, and i never thought i could be this sad, and i don't know why i'm writing this anymore, but i feel, with increasing intensity, that there's something about the story of morococha, that there's something about the story of morococha, that there's something about the story of morococha that i have to understand, that there's something about the story of morococha, that i have to understand

> porque el tiempo tiene grietas
> porque grietas tiene el alma

that there's something in the story of morococha that i have to understand, that we have to understand, that's why i'm still here, exploring each crevice in this prison cell, while the rain makes music against the ceiling

this urgency, to write, a recurrent feeling

how can i ever find peace?

this urgency to understand, to create a story, or a poem, that is relatable

perhaps, it's not about that, perhaps, it's just, it is what it is, es lo que hay

once again, the voices, lost, morococha, my babydaughter, my brother

    ¿qué nos queda?
    llorar no más

    ███████

in his quarry

    ¿qué nos queda?

    ¿qué nos queda?

you were in your mother's womb
when i started writing this book
now you're in kindergarten
learning how to read

i wonder what you'll say
when you read this

if you represent the struggle
then push

N.N.

"what do you do for a living papi?"

i make worlds mijo

i make worlds
with words

arriba no tenías lo que tienes aquí, pero la gente era feliz

era hermoso como se vivía acá

bingo bingo
lo perdí todo

sunday august 25th, 2013

supreme decree that declares a state of emergency in the district of morococha, in the province of yauli, in the department of junin

supreme decree n° 095-2013-pcm

todos somos hemos sido mineros

considering:

that, the district of morococha, in the province of yauli, in the department
of junin, is a mining town, whose exploitation activities date back to 1763
with a population according to the national institute of statistics and
informatics, of 4,884 inhabitants, the majority of which are mining
workers;

nos han cerrado nuestras escuelas

nos han quitado nuestros servicios

four boys play with their toy guns
right outside the municipality
in nueva morococha
around sunset
because play is necessary

that, according to technical report n° a 6636 geological danger in town of issued by the
mining and metallurgical geological institute - ingemmet, the area where mentioned town
morococha is located become exposed to mass movement mudslides, falling rocks and
landslides

play is necessary

        caused mainly by type material involved, absence vegetable coverage, excavated slopes
        adding to this the intense, the natural seismic, more so when such a is in an area of
        according to the seismic zonification map of peru, as well as vibrations by the from current
        mining activities

the more i study and talk to people and experts
the less i understand about the situation in morococha
and extractivism
in perú
and around the world

        as well as existence underground pits underneath the city, all of which
        coupled with quality of, makes location high-risk area

to arrive at a new language

    ¿qué va a ser de nuestro futuro, de nuestros hijos?

article 1. declaration state of emergency
the district morococha, the province of yauli, in department junin, is declared a state
emergency 60 days, due an imminent danger mass movements

no es como antes
ya no hay ese sentimiento de barrio ya
como una comunidad
es diferente
acá abajo

or perhaps
a story able to express
and contain
hold
the texture of reality
the lack of consistency

thursday october 24, 2o13

the problem between consonants

state of emergency extended in district morococha, province of, in the department

supreme decree
n° 116-2013-pcm

por un plato de lentejas se echan los peruanos

that supreme decree n° 116-2013-pcm, published october 24th, 2013, the emergency declared in of morococha, in the, by supreme decree n° 095-2013-PCM, extended for 60 days

sin plata no hay justicia

in order for entities involved in such, to continue carry out immediate necessary response rehabilitation actions as; as well as, as, as well as, the reduction minimization high risk existing, being, the main one, relocation population old town morococha

or perhaps
a story that refuses to

friday december 20th, 2013

state emergency extended in of morococha, of of yauli, in the, in the, in the

a story that refuses too

supreme decree n° 131-2013-pcm

she was so small
as i held her dead body
in the new mission bay hospital

this is not the way it should be

5 decretos supremos han sacado para que nos desaparezcan
5 decretos supremos han sacado para que nos desaparezcan

that, through supreem decree n° 095-2013-PCM published on 25th, 2013, the state
of declared, morococha, of the province, in the in the, in the, for sixty (60) days due

immminent danger mass movements

this is not the way it should be

no nos han escuchado, hemos estado en palacio de gobierno
¿cuántas veces hemos comido en la plaza san martín?
hemos comido en cartón, con nuestros hijos

and execution immediate necessary response rehabilitation action
destined reduce minimize existing high in the; as well as, as, among other
the, in the, relocation people living hazardous

she was so small
the rumor of a possibility
in that small, lifeless body

tuesday, november 4, 2014

supppreme decree approves the regulation article 3 of n° 30081, which
geographical capital of, in the province in the, department in the

porque antes morococha era un pueblo muy hospitalario

my daughter
ramona

        supreme decree
        n° 016-2014-vivienda

        considering:

like the dylan song
like my grandmother
mamameli

        that law n° 30081, which geographical location of district morococha, in of yauli, junín
        law n° 682 law creation district of

who died while i was
in my mother's womb
a sadness so familiar

       ¿qué cree señora que la voy a premiar porque se ha quedado?
       así me dijo el señor de la chinalco.

my father called me justiniano
when i was a kid
because i would often say
esto no es justo
esto no es justo

        determined capital city new morococha, as well as geographical location
        geographical coordinates:

this is not fair
this is not just

        el detalle es... así directamente, que quiero yo: que este pueblo sea respetado como tal, estos seres
        humanos que respiramos el aire, vemos el día y el anochecer

        384054 meters east 8 718 813 m north, utm projection
        datum wgs 1984, Z18

and i can't help but wonder
what does that even mean?

in order prevent safeguard the inhabitability residents of such

que seamos respetados como cualquier ser humano en cualquier parte del mundo, que tengan todos
sus derechos. Nada más, no queremos otra cosa.

why did a virus infect my baby's brain?
why did my brother kiko die of a heart attack
two weeks later while he was playing football in vietnam?
how do the people of morococha manage to keep going
even when faced with abuse and neglect and despair?

bingo bingo
lo perdí todo

pero cuando eso no sucede

no voy a ganar así vuelvo a jugar

what is this thing happening all the time always?

prevent safeguard inhabitability residents of such

but when that doesn't happen...

or perhaps

yo quiero trabajo
con trabajo
puedo educar a mis hijos

my research
not the books i read
or the notes i take
or the people i talk to

entre peruanos nos hicimos esto

prevent safeguard inhabitability residents of such

my research
what happens inside of me
when i read those books
and take those notes
and talk to those people

        ¿tú estás con la chinalco?

                prevent safeguard inhabitability residents of such

my research
inside of me
all the time
always

i cannot lose it

                                                bingo bingo

        ¿tú estás con la chinalco?

like ramona
and kiko

¿tú estás con la chinalco?

N.N.

i overheard two professors talking in the hallway the other day, one of them was saying that according to greek mythology, when castor and pollux invaded attica to liberate their sister helen, who had been taken by theseus, they threatened to destroy the city of athens. in order to avoid this, academus told castor and pollux where helen was hidden, and was revered as a hero. when the lacedaemonians invaded attica they spared his land because of this reason, and in this same land lay his burial site, which was adorned with olive plants. plato used to teach his students in this garden, which came to be known as academia.

in other words, the english term academic comes from a guy who was snitch, a narc, a rat, an opportunist who cashed in, somebody who didn't really want to get his hands dirty, but rather just tell everyone where things were located (helen in this case).

or the voice of the son, as imagined by the parent writer

i don't do it so they can call me bachelor or master or doctor

i don't do it because i want to listen to all those older white men talk for hours about their areas of expertise without ever acknowledging their power and their privilege and their entitlement

i don't do it so i can then turn around and "rightfully" claim my own place in all of this

i don't do it to be a broke-ass graduate student for like a decade

how shall i begin my story
that has no beginning
in these arroyos my great grandfather raised cattle
before the anglos ever came[1]

1. the opening monologue from the salt of the earth (1954); a film written by michael wilson and directed by herbert j. biberman.

y como yo digo siempre
aun muerta seguiré luchando

i do it because i like to fly

i do it because i want to be freedom

i do it because i believe "study is necessary for liberation"[1], and at so many levels

i do it because of the people of morococha

i do it because of your tío kiko, i miss him so much

i do it because of ramona

our roots go deep in this place
deeper than the pines
deeper than the mine shafts
this is my village

so it is better to speak
remembering

1. i'm pretty sure fred moten said this during a reading at ucsd in 2015, or i might've dreamt it. either way, i strongly believe he should be credited for the line.

we were never meant to survive[1]

i do it because i believe in what happens when people get together

and share

i do it because i believe in the struggle miqel

it's a question of resistance

> when i was a child it was called san marcos
> the anglos changed the name to zinc town
> zinc town, new mexico
> u – s – a
> this is our home

> *y como yo digo siempre*
> *aun muerta seguiré luchando*

i do it because it's always worth it

1. *litany for survival*, audre lorde.

even when it seems like it's not, especially when it seems like it's not

i do it because i don't want to compete and professionalize, compete and professionalize, compete and professionalize

i do it because i still believe in the public university, even after they suspended and fired so many of my colleagues and friends just for protesting in favor of a cost-of-living adjustment, even after they brought in the cops, once again, and brutalized the students

i still believe in the public university

and i believe higher education can be done without creating indebted beings

        the house is not ours
        but the flowers
        the flowers our ours

          so it is better to speak
          remembering
          we were never meant to survive

i do it because i don't give a fuck anymore, i don't give a fuck anymore, i do it because i don't give a fuck anymore, somewhere within the open pit i do it because i'm bookish and i like drugs, convoluted mechanisms of intellection and abstraction, why does the word academic have to be dirtied up in the process?

i do it because i want to change the way i feel towards the word academic

i do it because i like talking to people about the expansiveness of words, like objects, falling

i do it because i'm falling, like words

i do it because i'm bookish and i like drugs

you don't say good luck
you say don't give up

i do it because i don't believe the peruvian government when they said it was necessary to declare a state of emergency in morococha because of the "widespread protests and social unrest" which allowed the authorities to close down the schools and health centers and force the residents of morococha to relocate

i do it because of ███ and ████ and ███ and ███ and ███ and ████ and ███ and ████████ and all the residents of morococha that were kind enough to share their stories with me

i do it because i believe in their struggle

i believe in trying to make this world a better place for everyone, and not just for some

my name is esperanza

esperanza quintero
i am a miner's wife

y como yo digo siempre
aun muerta seguiré luchando

i do it because of you mijo

i do it because of you

i do it because i hope you'll want to try too, and struggle, and fight to make this world a better place for everyone, and not just for some

es injusto no tomar partido

i do it because i hope you'll want to, because it's always a choice

"but what if i don't want to struggle papi
what if i just want to surrender
and quietly go away?"

i would say that i love you, i love you, and i would say don't give up, don't give up, don't ever give up, and
i love you, i will always be here with you, don't give up, because there's so much love and beauty in the
world, and i'd be sad that i wasn't able to help you realize that it's always worth it, the struggle, it's always
worth it miqel, and it's necessary, it's necessary, but i would never hold it against you, because i love you, i
love you, don't give up, i will always be here with you, and it's a choice mijo, it's your choice

it's the fire
inside you

i do it because i hope you'll want to make that choice

i do it because i hope you'll always want to make that choice

so it is better to speak
remembering
we were never meant to survive

FLIGHT INSTRUCTIONS:

you and me
damon albarn

bread and butter
the roots

six days
dj shadow / mos def

amante bandido
miguel bosé

everything now
arcade fire

here comes the river
patrick watson

you can't stop me now
rza

king kunta
kendrick lamar

citizen cope
fame

everything is free
gillian welch

penny for a thought
saul williams

strange overtones
david byrne

puente
gustavo cerati

el amor acaba
jose jose

push
pharoahe monche

bingo bingo
jimmy whoo

the fire
the roots / john legend

and as i always say: even dead i'll keep fighting

*

that's why i was telling you

ask this person

ask that person
don't just rely on what i'm telling you
take from this person
take from that person
and come to your own conclusions

that's it

*

this hospital is killing me...
i don't know why they have me here

the morphine is killing me slowly
i want to be with my children
someone has to listen to us

we don't have enough money to get justice

*

as a mayor he had to fight for his town
money is stronger sometimes
and you humiliate others
look at us now

*

the mayor's office is a mine

*

we were better off before
when we had underground mining
chinalco is a cancer
this town should be thriving
someone has to tell our story
my son's first words:
ollanta traitor

*

chinalco workers are forbidden to buy what we here sell

*

out of indignation and so much fear
because it was too much abuse
my district was filled with police
you couldn't even walk
and there were no answers to give our children

i remember they called for a town meeting
and i stood in front of the authorities and i told them
enough with the abuse
this can't go on

because we're not criminals
we haven't violated anyone
much less killed anyone

let's unite together
someone has to hear us
someone has to know

and at midnight we were already leaving for lima
with our children
to protest
to make sure they hear us

and because we came to lima
the only thing, we didn't achieve much
but we made sure our town was demilitarized

and since i got into the struggle
i have suffered a lot because
it's not easy being a woman and leading a protest
because they kidnapped me
some police then they beat me up

and my son is, was born here
that's why i defend it
because of the injustice
so much fear
i became a rebel
and that's why i fight

before i didn't understand neither why to struggle
but when this arrived to my town
i understood a lot

i understood a lot and i got into the struggle
i put everything into this struggle

and as i always say
even dead i'll keep fighting

even dead
i'll keep fighting

*

don't be afraid neighbors
don't be afraid of the chinalco company

*

the voice of the people is the voice of god

we know who the guilty ones are

even the cops from here, defend the company

*

what's left for us?
crying, nothing else

what's left for us?

what's left for us?

*

up top you didn't have what you have here, but people were happy

it was beautiful how we lived here

*

we've all been miners

*

they have closed down our schools

they have closed down our utilities

*

what are we going to do? what's going to happen to our children?

*

it's not like before
there's no more neighborly feeling anymore
community like
it's different
down here

*

peruvians snitch on each other for a plate of lentils

*

without money there's no justice

*

they haven't listened to us, we've been in the government palace
how many times have we eaten in the san martin plaza?

we have eaten on cardboard, with our children

*

because morococha was a hospitable town before

*

what do you think lady that i'm going to award you because you stayed?
that's what the guy from chinalco told me

*

the thing is… what do i want: that this town be respected as such, these human beings that breathe
the air, watch the day and the sunset

*

that we be respected like any other human in any other part of the world. that we have all of our
rights, nothing else, we don't want something else

*

but when that doesn't happen…

*

but when that doesn't happen...

*

i want work
with work
i can educate my children

*

we did this amongst peruvians

*

are you with la chinalco?

*

are you with la chinalco?

*

are you with la chinalco?

*

and as i always say
even dead i'll keep fighting

*

and as i always say
even dead i'll keep fighting

*

and as i always say
even dead i'll keep fighting

First and foremost, I would like to thank the people of Morococha for being kind of enough to share their stories with me.[1] I hope this book does justice to your generosity, and I also hope it speaks to you somehow, as your stories have so intimately spoken to me. Thank you.

This project also began as a letter to my son Miqel; thank you for filling my life with the joy of parenting, this is for you mijo. I would also like to thank the rest of my family for always being there: Mom, Viejo, Susi, Kiko, Jaime, Isabela, Katerina, Makena, Lindsay. Thank you for believing in me, even when I don't.

The *open pit: a story about morococha and extractivism in the américas* has received considerable institutional support throughout the years, which has allowed me to take ample time to work on this project. I would like to thank the following institutions for their financial support: The Friends of the International Center (UCSD), The Humanities Institute (UCSC), The Idstrom Family Prize for Creative Writing (UCSC), and the University of California Dissertation Fellowship Program.

I would also like to thank the MFA in Writing Program at the University of California San Diego for their support while I was a student there. And perhaps more specifically to Cristina Rivera-Garza, Rae

1. The passages in italics throughout the *open pit* correspond to the testimonies of the residents of Morococha, whom I talked to between 2014 and 2019, these conversations were in Spanish. I have translated their testimonies into English in the last section of the book, titled "testimonios".

Armantrout, Ben and Sandra Doller, Anna-Joy Springer, Curtis Marez, Tania Mayer and John Granger for their invaluable comments and guidance. Similarly, I would like to thank the PhD in Literature Program at the University of California Santa Cruz, and the Creative-Critical concentration within that program. I am extremely grateful for the generous advice and support I received from Micah Perks, Ronaldo Wilson, Juan Poblete, Chris Chen, Karen Tei Yamashita, Eric Porter, and Larry Andrews.

I would also like to thank my colleagues at both UCSD and UCSC, whose input throughout the years has been instrumental for the completion of this project: Kendall Grady, Brett Zehner, Ben Segal, Omar Pimienta, Pepe Rojo, Ethan Sparks, Gabe Kalmuss-Katz, Cathy Thomas, Whitney DeVos, Gabriela Ramírez, Eric Sneathen, Jared Harvey, Nicholas Wittington, Stephen Richter and Jackson Kroopf.

And to the folks in Peru who have supported this project in concrete and immaterial ways: Giancarlo Huapaya, Mariel García, Marisol de la Cadena, Eloy Neira, Víctor Vich, Luciana Córdova, Carlos Contreras, Jorge Runcie Tanaka, and many more I'm probably forgetting at this moment. I would also like to thank Arturo Higa Taira from Álbum del Universo Bakterial for his continuous support throughout the years, and likewise to Rafael Espinosa for his mentorship.

Sections of this book have been published in the following literary journals: *The Hostos Review*, *Entropy*, *Free State Review*, *Flag + Void*, and *The Florida Review* at UCF. I would like to thank the editors of these journals for believing in this project. And to Tim Roberts, Julie Carr, and the folks at Counterpath. Thank you for your trust and all of your work, I can't think of a better home for this book.

And finally, I would like to thank the people of Morococha once more. Gracias por todo, y disculpen la eterna demora.

Sebastián Rodríguez (Huancayo, 1896 – Morococha, 1968) portrays a historical change through his photography: the violent and silent modernization process of the Andean communities in Peru's central mountain region, which were impacted by the territorial affirmation of corporate capitalism during the period between world wars. Precisely there, where the State doesn't exist, and over the remains of the existing feudality and coloniality, order is structured by the transnational extractive company. The identification photos, intended to fulfill a bureaucratic role of labor control, are witness to such displacement and showcase, contradictorily, an arresting helplessness and dignity in the young adults, women and men who were recorded; due to the care, respect, and empathy with which they were photographed.

That similarity, between the folks expelled from society and their own territories because of the structural violence and the political violence of the 1930s and 1980s, is precisely what drives my interpolations. For this project, I engage in the appropriation, citation, and photographic displacement of Sebastian Rodriguez's portraits, which allows me to speak here and now about folks victimized by the "violence of time." The real Peruvian gold is not the metal extracted from the Andes, it's the indigenous people themselves, ignored and deferred by the exploitation and ransacking of their selves and their territory. To fight for the recovery of a memory that gives back the dignity that was taken from them and reconstructs a collective body which is missing and sequestered by the force of violence, this is the motivation underlying this and other projects I carry out.

—Alfredo Márquez. 2016.